I0797673

Junk Food for Thought

Favorite Fictional Foods

Kenny Abdo

Fly!
An Imprint of Abdo Zoom
abdobooks.com

abdobooks.com

Published by Abdo Zoom, a division of ABDO, P.O. Box 398166, Minneapolis, Minnesota 55439.

Printed in the United States of America, North Mankato, Minnesota.
052025
092025

Photo Credits: Alamy, AP Images, Everett Collection, Getty Images, Pond5, Shutterstock, ©Famartin p.cover / CC BY-SA 4.0
Production Contributors: Kenny Abdo, Jennie Forsberg, Grace Hansen
Design Contributors: Candice Keimig, Neil Klinepier, Laura Graphenteen

Library of Congress Control Number: 2024947737

Publisher's Cataloging-in-Publication Data

Names: Abdo, Kenny, author.
Title: Favorite fictional foods / by Kenny Abdo
Description: Minneapolis, Minnesota : Abdo Zoom, 2026 | Series: Junk food for thought | Includes online resources and index.
Identifiers: ISBN 9781098288785 (lib. bdg.) | ISBN 9781098289485 (ebook) | ISBN 9781098289836 (Read-to-me ebook)
Subjects: LCSH: Junk food--Juvenile literature. | Food technology--Juvenile literature. | Food additives--Juvenile literature. | Food in popular culture-Juvenile literature. | Processed foods--Juvenile literature.
Classification: DDC 641.3--dc23

TABLE OF CONTENTS

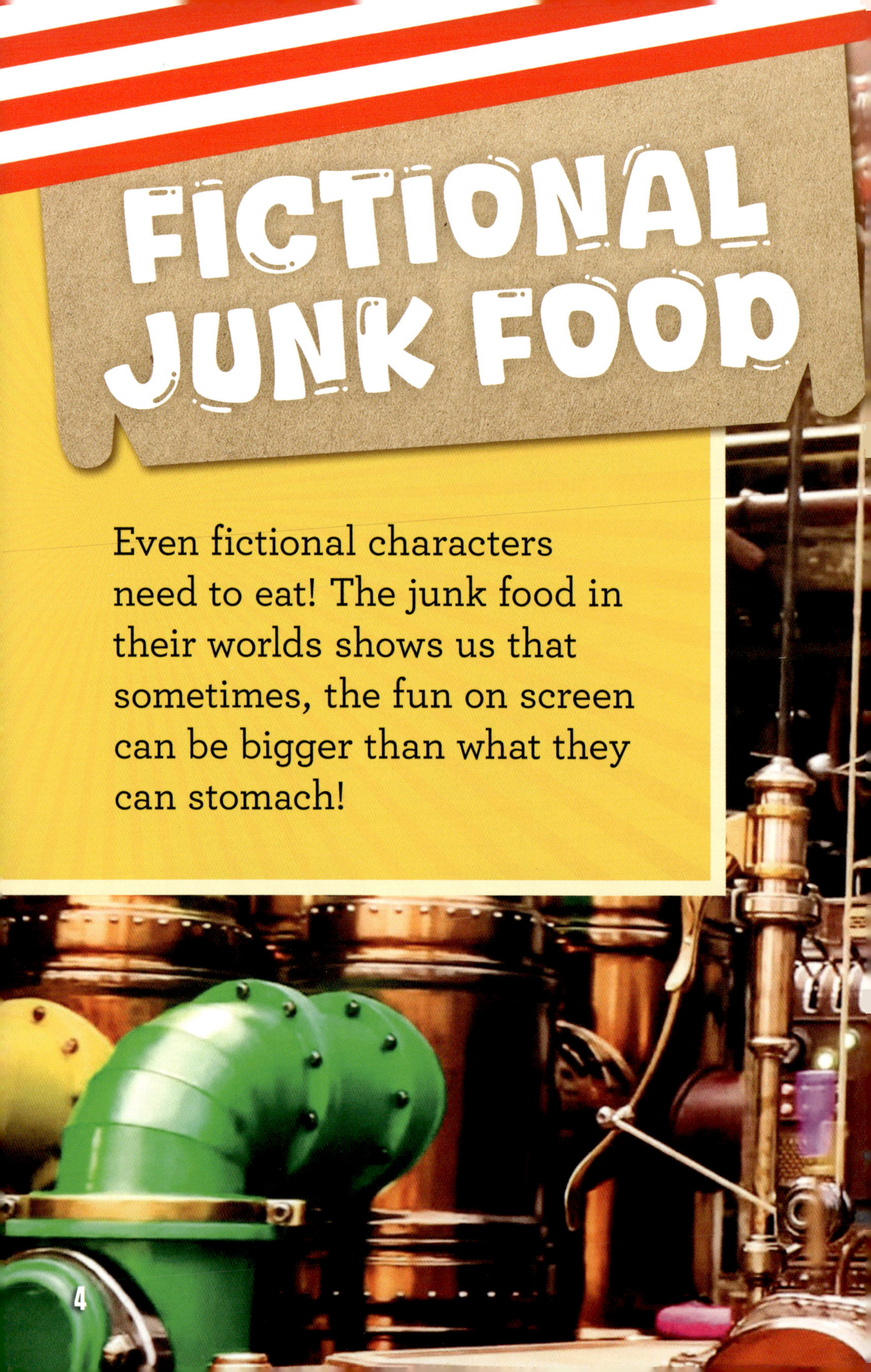

FICTIONAL JUNK FOOD

Even fictional characters need to eat! The junk food in their worlds shows us that sometimes, the fun on screen can be bigger than what they can stomach!

THE EARLY JUNK

One of the first fictional foods to jump off the page and into stomachs came from a wonderland. Lewis Carroll used food in *Alice in Wonderland* to share his views on hunger in **Victorian** society. With fun treats like Jello, pocket watch cookies, and caterpillar kabobs, readers went mad with cravings!

10/6

In 1960, Dr. Seuss introduced *Green Eggs and Ham* to kids everywhere. This dish quickly became a favorite among readers. Dr. Seuss and his green breakfast sparked imagination and appetites around the world!

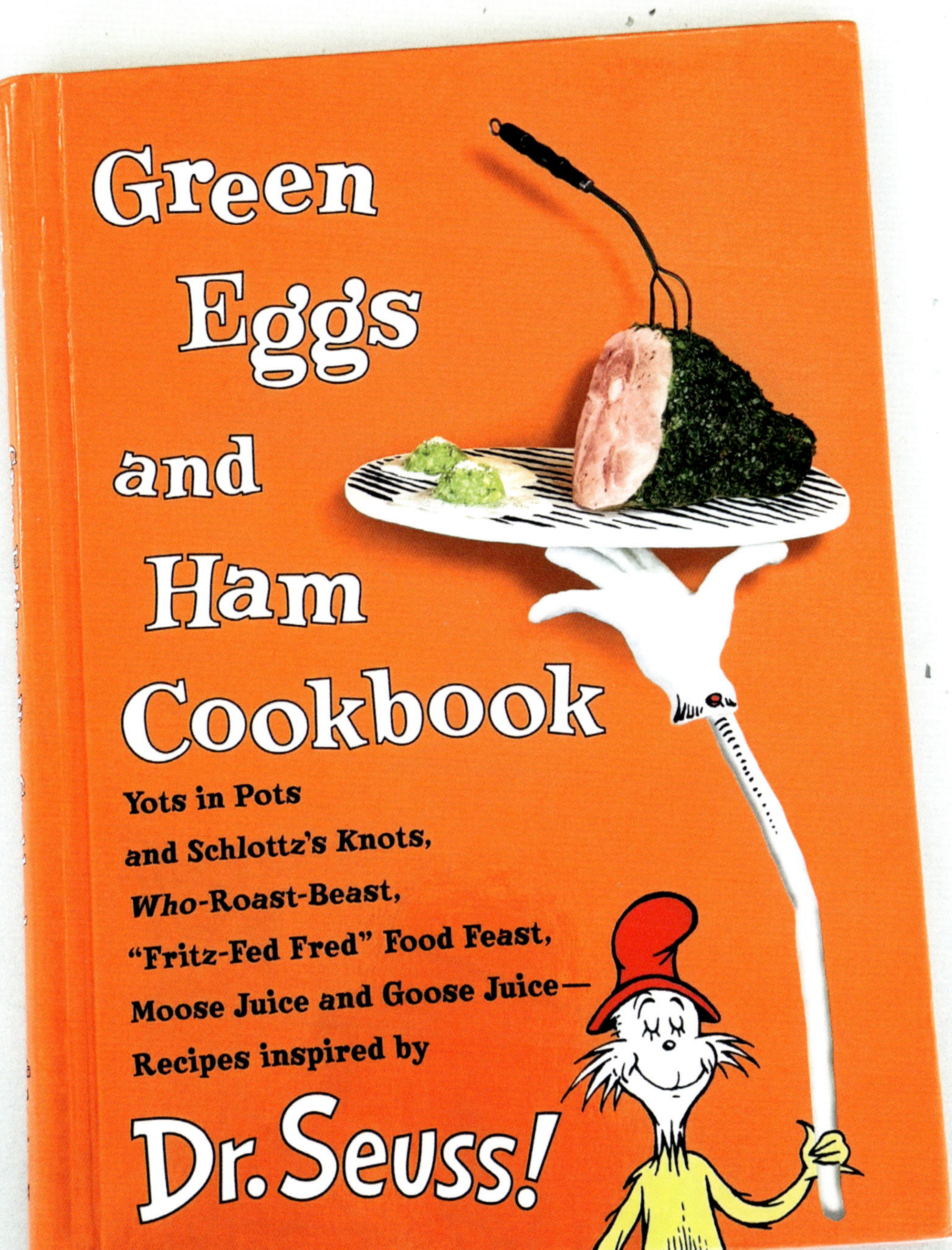
Green Eggs and Ham Cookbook
Yots in Pots
and Schlottz's Knots,
Who-Roast-Beast,
"Fritz-Fed Fred" Food Feast,
Moose Juice and Goose Juice—
Recipes inspired by
Dr. Seuss!

THE FOOD PROCESS JUNK

Each episode of *The Flintstones* began the same. A giant rack of dinosaur ribs was attached to the family's car and tipped it over. The show also featured the popular Bronto Burger. During the 1960s, *The Flintstones* gave fans laughs and dino-sized cravings!

Bill's
CANDY SHOP
ALL
WONK
CHOCOLA
WONK
fudge malk
NKA'S

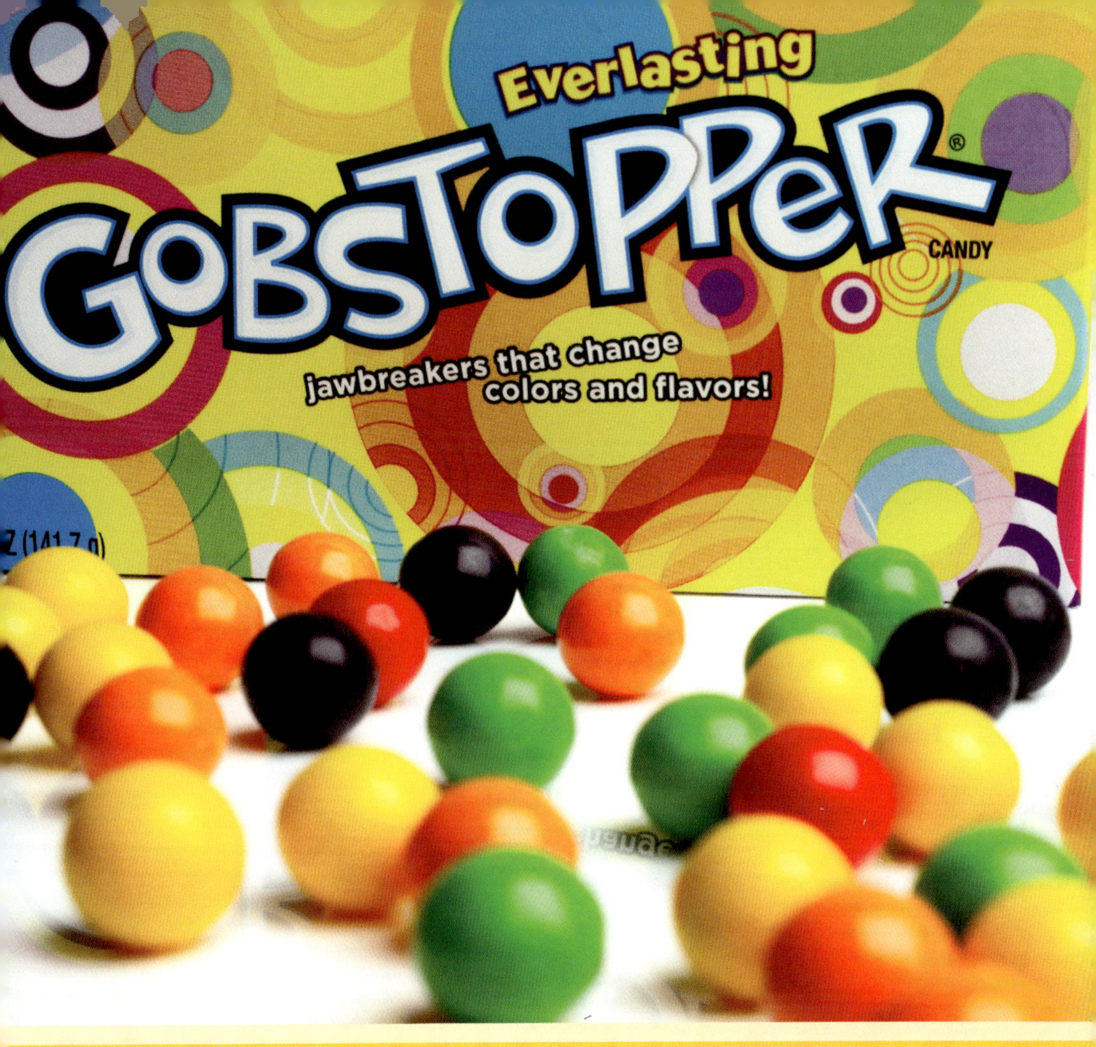

Willy Wonka & the Chocolate Factory featured many tasty treats. But the Everlasting Gobstopper stood out the most. The candy that never ran out was a dream for any kid who loved sweets. In 1976, kids got to enjoy this treat in real life when it **debuted** on shelves!

Scooby Snacks have fueled the Mystery Inc. team since 1969. These magical treats gave Shaggy and his pup the energy to solve mysteries. In fact, these fictional bites became so popular that a real version was unleashed in 2005!

SCOOBY
SNACKS

In 1977, blue milk became all the rage throughout the galaxy after Luke Skywalker poured himself a glass. Sci-fi fans were instantly captivated. In 2019, the humans of Earth got to try it at Disneyland's Star Wars: Galaxy's Edge!

Homer Simpson loves only one thing more than his family. Since *The Simpsons* first aired in 1989, Homer's passion for donuts became a running joke on the show, while making fans crave the d'oh-nuts!

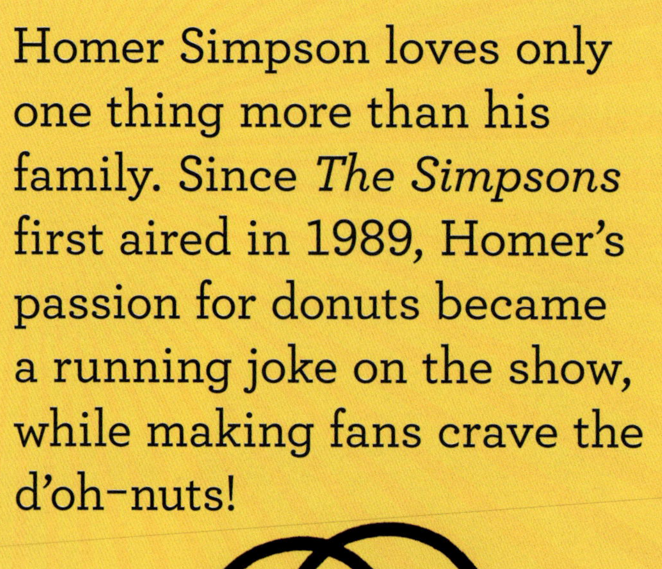

MOONLINER
Coca-Cola
ing Refreshment to a Thirsty Galaxy

In 1995's *Toy Story*, Pizza Planet offered tasty pizza and redemption. It was featured in every movie in the series after. The fictional pizza joint became real in 1995 at Disney's Hollywood Studios. Another opened at Disneyland in 1998.

The first Krabby Patty was fried up in *SpongeBob SquarePants* in 1999. The veggie burger, cooked by SpongeBob, has a secret recipe making it special.

Everyone from Bikini Bottom to **landlubbers** have fallen in love! The fast-food **chain** Wendy's unwrapped a real Krabby Patty in 2024.

Butterbeer first sweetened the pages of *Harry Potter* in 2001. The drink, made with butterscotch, cream soda, and whipped cream, warmed up Hogwarts students after chilly **Quidditch** games. Today, any muggle can conjure up a mug at Universal Studios!

THE WIZARDING WORLD OF
Harry Potter
AT UNIVERSAL ORLANDO® RESORT

THE TUMMY ACHE

Many fans love making their favorite fictional foods at home. Popular YouTuber Andrew Rea shares these recipes on his channel, *Binging with Babish*. He shows how to **recreate** beloved snacks in your kitchen!

POP CORN

From green breakfast to ratatouille made by rodents, fictional junk food has fed pop culture's hungriest, most iconic characters and our imaginations!

GLOSSARY

chain – restaurants that serve food quickly and efficiently. They typically have a regular menu and focus on convenience, with many locations throughout the country.

debut – a first appearance.

landlubber – an insult used by pirates toward someone not comfortable or experienced at sea. Pirates often look down on landlubbers due to their lack of sailing skills.

Quidditch – the main sport of the Harry Potter world. Players ride broomsticks and score points by throwing balls through hoops. The game ends when a player catches the Golden Snitch.

recreation – a new version or copy of something, made to resemble the original.

Victorian era – referring to the era from 1837 to 1901 when Queen Victoria reigned over Great Britain and Ireland. This time saw quick industrial growth, but it also created a lot of poverty and hunger for the working class.

JUNK FOOD FOR THOUGHT

ONLINE RESOURCES

To learn more about fictional food, please visit abdobooklinks.com or scan this QR code. These links are routinely monitored and updated to provide the most current information available.

INDEX